Come In

by Katie Bristol   illustrated by Kristin Barr

⦿ Harcourt
SCHOOL PUBLISHERS

ISBN 10 0-15-364050-2
ISBN 13 978-0-15-364050-6

2 3 4 5 6 7 8 9 10   179   17 16 15 14 13 12 11 10 09 08

Ordering Options
ISBN 10 0-15-364151-7
ISBN 13 978-0-15-364151-0

Tim can sit.

Come in, Tim.

Pam can come in.

Sid can come in.

Come in, Tim.

Tim can come in.

Tim did come in!

School-Home Connection Ask your child to read the book to you. Then talk about a time when your child tried to do something he or she was nervous about doing.

Come In
Word Count: 27

High-Frequency Words

come

Decodable Words*

can	**Sid**
did	**sit**
in	**Tim**
Pam	

Boldface words indicate sound-spelling introduced in this story.

Harcourt
SCHOOL PUBLISHERS
www.harcourtschool.com

ISBN-13: 978-0-15-364050-6
ISBN-10: 0-15-364050-2

9 780153 640506

90000>